GW00708255

This book belongs to

_____

Chicken Soup for the Soul®
Stories to Warm a
Mother's Heart

VERMILION
LONDON

First published by Andrews McMeel Publishing, Kansas City.
This edition published in 2000 by Vermilion,
an imprint of Ebury Press, Random House,
20 Vauxhall Bridge Road, London SW1V 2SA
www.randomhouse.co.uk

The Random House Group Limited Reg. No. 954009

Papers used by Vermilion are natural, recyclable products
made from wood grown in sustainable forests

Printed in Italy by Graphicom

A CIP catalogue record for this book is available from the
British Library

ISBN 0-09-182567-9

Chicken Soup for the Soul® Stories to Warm a Mother's Heart

Inspired by the international bestseller

Chicken Soup for the **Soul**®

by Jack Canfield and Mark Victor Hansen

Second ♥ Skin

By Caroline Castle Hicks

My favorite pair of old jeans will never fit me again. I have finally accepted this immutable truth. After nurturing and giving birth to two babies, my body has undergone a metamorphosis. I may have returned to my pre-baby weight, but subtle shifts and expansions have taken place — my own version of continental drift. As a teenager, I never understood the difference between junior and misses sizing; misses clothing just looked old. Now it is all too clear that wasp waists and micro-fannies are but the fleeting trappings of youth. But that's okay, because while the jeans no longer button, the life I exchanged for them fits better than they ever did.

For me, this is a barefoot, shorts and T-shirt time of life. I have slipped so easily into young motherhood; it is the most comfortable role I have ever worn. No rough seams, no snagging zippers. Just a feeling that I have stepped out of the dressing room in something that finally feels right.

I love the feel of this baby on my hip, his soft head a perfect fit under my chin, his tiny hands splayed out like small pink starfish against my arms. I love the way my eight-year-old daughter walks alongside us as we cross the grocery store's sunny parking lot. On gorgeous spring days, the breeze lifts her wispy ponytail, and we laugh at how the sunshine makes the baby sniff and squint. I am constantly reaching out to touch them, the way a seamstress would two lengths of perfect silk, envisioning what might be made from them, yet hesitant to alter them, to lose the weight of their wholeness in my hands.

On those rare mornings when I wake up before they do, I go into their rooms and watch them sleeping, their faces creased and rosy. Finally, they squirm and stretch themselves awake, reaching out for a hug. I gather them up, bury my face in them and breathe deeply. They are like towels just pulled from the dryer, tumbled warm and cottony.

Sometimes, I follow the sound of girlish voices to my daughter's room, where she and her friends play dress-up, knee-deep in garage-sale chiffon, trying life on for size. Fussing and preening in front of the mirror, they drape themselves in cheap beads and adjust tiaras made of sequins and cardboard. I watch these little girls with their lank, shiny hair that no rubber bands or barrettes seem able to tame. They are constantly pushing errant strands behind their ears, and in that grown-up gesture, I see glimpses of the women they will become. I know that too soon these clouds of organdy and lace will settle permanently into their battered boxes, the ones that have served as treasure chests and princess thrones. They will become the hand-me-downs of my daughter's girlhood, handed back to me.

For now, though, my children curl around me on the sofa in the evening, often falling asleep, limbs limp and soft against me like the folds of a well-worn nightgown. For now, we still adorn each other, and they are content to be clothed in my embrace. I know there will be times that will wear like scratchy wool sweaters and four-inch heels. We will have to try on new looks together, tugging and scrunching, trying to keep the basic fabric intact. By then, we will have woven a complicated tapestry with its own peculiar pattern, its snags and pulls and tears.

But I will not forget this time, of drowsy heads against my shoulder, of footy pajamas and mother-daughter dresses, of small hands clasped in mine. This time fits me. I plan to wear it well.

13

Let's Go

Bug

Hunting

More Often

By Barbara Chesser, Ph.D.

One fall afternoon I rushed home from the university where I taught. I prepared a hasty dinner, threatened my nine-year-old daughter, Christi, to hurry and finish her homework "or else," and properly reprimanded Del, my husband, for leaving his dusty shoes on the good carpet. I then frantically vacuumed the entryway because a group of prestigious ladies were coming by to pick up some good used clothing for a worthwhile cause; and then later a graduate student would be at our house to work on a very important thesis — one that I was certain would make a sound contribution to research.

As I paused to catch my breath, I heard Christi talking with a friend on the telephone. Her comments went something like this: "Mom is cleaning house — some ladies we don't even know are coming by to pick up some old worn-out clothes... and a college student is coming out to work on a thesis... no, I don't know what a thesis is... I just know Mom isn't doing anything important... and she won't go bug hunting with me."

Before Christi had hung up the phone, I had put on my jeans and old tennis shoes, persuaded Del to do likewise, pinned a note to the door telling the graduate student I'd be back soon, and set the box of used clothing on the front porch with a note on it that Del, Christi and I had gone bug hunting.

A Mother's Love

By David Giannelli

I am a New York City fireman. Being a fire-fighter has its grim side. When someone's business or home is destroyed, it can break your heart. You see a lot of terror and some-times even death. But the day I found Scarlett was different. That was a day about life. And love.

It was a Friday. We'd responded to an early morning alarm in Brooklyn at a burning garage. As I was getting my gear on, I heard the sound of cats crying. I couldn't stop—I would have to look for the cats after the fire was put out.

This was a large fire, so there were other

hook and ladder companies there as well. We
had been told that everyone in the building
had made it out safely. I sure hoped so — the
entire garage was filled with flames, and it
would have been futile for anyone to attempt
a rescue anyway. It took a long time and many
firefighters to finally bring the enormous blaze
under control.

At that point I was free to investigate the
cat noises, which I still heard. There con-
tinued to be a tremendous amount of smoke
and intense heat coming from the building. I
couldn't see much, but I followed the meowing
to a spot on the sidewalk about five feet away
from the front of the garage. There, crying and

huddled together, were three terrified little kittens. Then I found two more, one in the street and one across the street. They must have been in the building, as their fur was badly singed. I yelled for a box and out of the crowd around me, one appeared. Putting the five kittens in the box, I carried them to the porch of a neighboring house.

I started looking for a mother cat. It was obvious that the mother had gone into the burning garage and carried each of her babies, one by one, out to the sidewalk. Five separate trips into that raging heat and deadly smoke — it was hard to imagine. Then she had attempted to get them across the street, away from the building. Again, one at a time. But she hadn't been able to finish the job. What had happened to her?

A cop told me he had seen a cat go into a vacant lot near where I'd found the last two kittens. She was there, lying down and crying. She was horribly burnt: her eyes were blistered shut, her paws were blackened, and her fur was singed all over her body. In some places you could see her reddened skin show-ing through the burned fur. She was too weak to move anymore. I went over to her slowly, talking gently as I approached. I figured that she was a wild cat and I didn't want to alarm her. When I picked her up, she cried out in pain, but she didn't struggle. The poor animal reeked of burnt fur and flesh. She gave me a look of utter exhaustion and then relaxed in my arms as much as her pain would allow. Sensing her trust in me, I felt my throat tighten and the tears start in my eyes. I was determined to save this brave little cat and her family. Their lives were, literally, in my hands.

I put the cat in the box with the mewing kittens. Even in her pathetic condition, the blinded mother circled in the box and touched each kitten with her nose, one by one, to make sure they were all there and all safe. She was content, in spite of her pain, now that she was sure the kittens were all accounted for.

These cats obviously needed immediate medical care. I thought of a very special animal shelter out on Long Island, the North Shore Animal League, where I had taken a severely burned dog I had rescued eleven years earlier. If anyone could help them, they could.

I called to alert the Animal League that I was on my way with a badly burned cat and her kittens. Still in my smoke-stained fire gear, I drove my truck there as fast as I could. When I pulled into the driveway, I saw two teams of vets and technicians standing in the parking lot waiting for me. They whisked the cats into a treatment room — the mother on a table with one vet team and all the kittens on another table with the second team.

Utterly exhausted from fighting the fire, I stood in the treatment room, keeping out of the way. I didn't have much hope that these cats would survive. But somehow, I just couldn't leave them. After a long wait, the vets told me they would observe the kittens and their mother overnight, but they weren't very optimistic about the mother's chances of survival.

I returned the next day and waited and waited. I was about to completely give up hope when the vets finally came over to me. They told me the good news — the kittens would survive.

"And the mother?" I asked. I was afraid to hear the reply.

It was still too early to know.

I came back every day, but each day it was the same thing: they just didn't know. About a week after the fire, I arrived at the shelter in a bleak mood, thinking, *Surely if the mother cat was going to make it, she'd have come around by now. How much longer could she hover between life and death?* But when I walked in the door, the vets greeted me with big smiles and gave me the thumbs-up sign! Not only was she going to be all right — in time she'd even be able to see again.

Now that she was going to live, she needed a

name. One of the technicians came up with the name Scarlett, because of her reddened skin.

Knowing what Scarlett had endured for her kittens, it melted my heart to see her reunited with them. And what did mama cat do first? Another head count! She touched each of her kittens again, nose to nose, to be sure they were all still safe and sound. She had risked her life, not once, but five times – and it had paid off. All of her babies had survived.

As a firefighter, I see heroism every day. But what Scarlett showed me that day was the height of heroism — the kind of bravery that comes only from a mother's love.

When Did She Really Grow Up?

By Beverly Beckham

Every night after I tucked her into bed, I sang to her, a silly song, a made-up song, our song. "Stay little, stay little, little little stay; little stay little stay little."

She would giggle and I would smile. The next morning I would say: "Look at you. You grew. The song didn't work."

I sang that song for years, and every time I finished, she crossed her heart and promised she wouldn't grow any more.

Then one night, I stopped singing it. Who knows why. Maybe her door was closed. Maybe she was studying. Maybe she was on the phone talking to someone. Or maybe I realized it was time to give her permission to grow.

It seems to me now that our song must have had some magic because all the nights I sang it, she remained a baby... four, five, six, seven, eight, nine, ten. They felt the same. They even looked the same. She got taller and her feet got bigger and some teeth fell out and new ones grew in, but she still had to be reminded to brush them and her hair and to take a shower every now and then.

She played with dolls and Play-Doh. Though Candy Land was abandoned for Monopoly and Clue, across a table, there she still was. For years, she was like those wooden dolls that nest one inside the other, identical in everything but size.

Or at least that's how I saw her. She roller-skated and ice-skated and did cartwheels in shopping malls and blew bubbles and drew pictures, which we hung on the refrigerator. She devoured Yodels and slushes and woke early on Sunday mornings to watch *Davey and Goliath.*

She never slept through the night, not at ten months, not at ten years. When she was small, she'd wake and cry and I'd take her into bed with me. When she got bigger, she'd wake and make her way down the hall, and in the morning, I would find her lying beside me.

She used to put notes under my pillow before she went to bed. I used to put notes in her bologna sandwiches before she went to school. She used to wait by the phone when I was away. I used to wait at the bus stop for her to come home.

The song, the notes, the waking up to find her next to me, the waiting at the bus stop — all these things ended a long time ago. Upstairs now is a young woman, a grown-up. She has been grown up for a while. Everyone else has seen this — everyone but me.

I look at her today, one week before she graduates from high school, and I am proud of her, proud of the person she has become. But

I'm sad, too — not for her, but for me. There has been a child in this house for twenty-five years. First one grew up, then the other, but there was always this one...the baby.

Now the baby is grown. And despite what people tell me — you don't lose them, they go away but they come home again, you'll like the quiet when she's gone, the next part of life is the best — I know that what lies ahead won't be like what was.

I loved what was. I loved it when she toddled into my office and set up her toy typewriter next to mine. I loved watching her run down the hall at nursery school straight into my arms, after a separation of just two-

and-a-half hours. I loved taking her to buy stickers and for walks and to movies. I loved driving her to gymnastics and listening to her friends. I loved being the one she raced to when she was happy or frightened or sad. I loved being the center of her world.

"Mommy, come play with me."

"Mommy, I'm home."

"Mommy, I love you the bestest and the widest."

What replaces these things?

"Want to see my cap and gown?" she says now, peeking into my office. She holds it up. She smiles. She's happy. I'm happy for her. She kisses me on the cheek and says, "I love you, Mom." And then she walks upstairs.

I sit at my desk and though my heart hurts, I smile. I think what a privilege motherhood is, and how very lucky I am.

True Beauty

By Charlotte Ward

For Mother's Day, Jeannie had put considerable effort and planning into buying something very special for her mother, Bess. She had carefully put together the cost of an image consultation gift certificate out of her first few paychecks. On the appointed day, this young daughter brought her shy, plain mother to my studio.

During the color draping and makeover, Bess confessed that she had concentrated on her family for years and ignored herself. Consequently she had never even considered what clothes looked good on her or how to apply her makeup.

As I placed pretty colors close to her face, she began to blossom, though she didn't seem to realize it. After applying the finishing touches of blush and lipstick to enhance her coloring, I invited her to view herself in the big cheval mirror. She took a long look, as if she were surveying a stranger, then edged closer and closer to her image. Finally, staring open-mouthed, she touched the mirror lightly. "Jeannie," she motioned, "come here." Drawing her daughter beside her, she pointed toward the image. "Jeannie, look at me. I'm beautiful!"

The young woman smiled at the older woman in the mirror with tears in her eyes. "Yes, Mother, you have always been — beautiful."

39

Sending Kids Off to School

By Susan Union

I could see how the scene was going to play itself out as clearly as if it had been written in a movie script.

"Five more minutes, honey, then we have to leave," I called to my five-year-old daughter, who had been frolicking in the Pacific Ocean for the past hour. It was a partial truth. Although I did have a million things to do that day, I decided to collect my child when I saw that she had found some older kids to frolic with. They were bigger and stronger, and the waves didn't knock them down as easily as they did my daughter. With exuberant five-year-old confidence, she kept following them out farther and farther toward the breaking waves. She was a proficient pool swimmer, but the deep blue sea was a different matter.

Maybe she didn't hear me calling her name above the roar of the ocean; maybe she did hear and was just ignoring me — it was impossible to tell. It had been an impromptu trip to the beach, so I wasn't wearing my swimsuit. Reluctantly, I hiked up my shorts and plunged into the ocean. Even in August I drew in a sharp breath as the water came in contact with my thighs.

"Hey, time's up, we have to go now." She turned, gave me a "See ya, Mom" look and headed farther into the surf. I splashed out

and grabbed her arm. My shorts were soaked.
I wondered if anyone was watching our little
drama unfold.

"No!" she screamed, "I don't want to
leave!" (Why is it that kids never want to get
out of the water?) She jerked her arm away
from me and pushed her defiant little body
closer to Tokyo. I could see the headline now:
"Child drowns while pursued by irate mother."

Now she was in over her head. Overcome
with fear and rage I grabbed her, firmly this
time, and began to drag her out. She did not
come willingly. She screamed more intensely
with every breath. It didn't stop when we got
on shore. She wriggled and kicked, struggling

violently in the sand to rid herself of me and charge back into the water. Now people were staring. I didn't care. I had to get her far enough away so that she couldn't plunge back into the powerful waves. She screamed and thrashed about like a wild animal caught in a trap, growling and scratching. The gritty sand clung to our wet skin.

By now I was shaking. I could hardly believe what happened next. A firm believer in nonviolent discipline — until now, that is — I smacked her on the bottom, hard. It stunned her enough to make her freeze and stop her hysterical ravings. She stood there almost completely covered in sand and with her mouth wide open, unable to take a breath.

"Come on!" I said through clenched teeth as I pulled her along toward the path that would lead us away from the beach. She hopped alongside of me, seething and jibbering. I realized she was trying to tell me something. Her unintelligible words alternated with jagged sobs as she shifted her weight from one foot to another. Her feet! Now that we were out of the surf, the sand was scalding hot. I had been clutching her thongs all along. "I'm so sorry, sweetie. Put these on." I slipped her thongs on her trembling feet, then we climbed the path toward the car and headed home.

That was weeks ago. Now it was September,

and I was back on the beach, alone. This time the sand was cool. It yielded softly beneath my feet as I walked along the edge of the receding water line. The morning sun had not been up long enough to work its magic. As I walked the beach, tears welled up in my eyes. I could see the image of my daughter earlier that morning, heading into her freshly painted kindergarten classroom for her first day of school. Her new day pack was slung proudly over her shoulder. The design of yellow and purple puppies and kittens verified her tender years.

I'd driven straight to the beach after dropping her off. There was something so reassuring in the never-ending cresting and breaking of the waves. I hoped the pounding surf would soothe my anxious thoughts.

"I love you, Mommy!" she had called out cheerfully from the window as I walked back to my car.

"I'll pick you up after school," I called back. I turned to blow her a kiss, but she had already turned from the window.

I had dreamed of this day for years — five to be exact. I dreamed of this day soon after I brought her home from the hospital. I tried holding her, rocking her, and singing to her. When all that failed, I would give her a bottle, her "binky," her bear... anything.

I dreamed of this day when she was only a year old and she spent her days lurching through the house unsteadily, learning to walk. I was so concerned that she might maim herself, I followed her around, hovering with arms outstretched like a giant bear. There was the time she ran smack into the corner of a door at full toddler speed. The blood gushed like a fountain from above her eye, but she was much more calm and brave about having it stitched than I was.

When she was two, I needed a break from full-time mommyhood badly. I had never been away from her for even one night. But there I was, halfway around the world in Austria. I had left her with my parents and had finally taken my break. But when I heard her tiny little voice over the long-distance phone lines, my voice cracked so badly that I could hardly answer her back.

And this past summer, our days on end of being constantly together caused her to demand my unfailing attention. As the summer's heat grew more oppressive, I got listless but she became more spirited. She wanted more of everything – more pool time, more ice cream, more Popsicles, more playtime, more of me. Every day I heard, "Mom, let's go to the park, let's go to the beach, let's go to the Wild Animal Park, let's go, let's go, let's go!"

Why the tears then? I stopped walking and sat on a rough outcropping of rocks, on a lovely beach on a glorious day feeling miserable. I watched the seagulls wheel and dive, their constant motion distracting the thoughts running through my mind.

I should be happy, I thought. No more incessant chatter bombarding me twelve hours a day. Now I could think free, uncluttered thoughts in a stream of connected ideas. I would be free to go back to school or start the business I'd been thinking about. I could have lunch with friends at restaurants that didn't hand out crayons and coloring menus as you were seated. I could go shopping by myself without having my daughter stand in the middle of the clothing carousels spinning the rack, perilously close to tipping it over while the sales clerk glared with disapproval. I could roll up the windows in my car, pick a CD that wasn't Raffi or Barney and sing at the top of my lungs without hearing her say, "Don't sing, Mommy! Don't sing!" I could even go to the grocery store without having to deal with bribery and blackmail.

The truth is, I'd miss having her by my side. I'd become used to having a constant companion for the past five years. "Don't worry, Mom, we'll still have our afternoons together," she had reassured me at the breakfast table that morning.

With that thought in mind, I collected my things off the beach and headed for my car. It was time to go pick up my baby — oh, my kindergartner — from her first day of school. I was looking forward to spending the afternoon together.

53

Mother's Day

By Sharon Nicola Cramer

One day while in my early 30s, I sat in a Midwestern church and burst into tears. It was Mother's Day, and ladies of all shapes and sizes, young and old, were being applauded by their families and the whole congregation. Each received a lovely rose and returned to the pews, where I sat empty-handed. Sorry to my soul, I was convinced I had missed my chance at that great adventure, that selective sorority called "motherhood."

All that changed one February when, pushing 40 and pushing with all my might, I brought forth Gabriel Zacharias. It took 24 hours of labor for me to produce that little four-pound, eight-ounce bundle of joy. No wonder those ladies got flowers!

Any mother who has survived one birth amazes herself at her willingness to go for two. Jordan Raphael was born the following March. He was smaller and labor was shorter; but I still felt I deserved flowers.

The sorority I joined requires an extended hazing period: nine months of demanding cravings for unusual foods you can't keep down; weight gain you can't explain; a walk that is part buffalo and part duck; unique bedtime constructions of pillows designed to support this bulge and fill in that gap but avoid all pressure on the bladder; and extensive stretch marks culminating in excruciating labor pain.

With labor, the hazing period ends. But with the child's birth, the initiation period in this great sorority has just begun. The painful tugs on the heart strings far exceed whatever physical pain labor required. There was my older son's first cut that drew blood, his spiked fevers, his long bout with pneumonia; my younger son's terror at a big barking dog, his near-miss with a car, the death of his pet rat.

While the hazing period may seem over-long, this initiation period never ends. I wake up when my sons cough. I hear their teddy bears land with a soft thud on the floor next to their beds. In the supermarket I respond to children calling "Mo-ther!" and the kids, I realize, aren't even my own!

I've advanced past bottle weaning, potty training, the first days of school and the first trip to the dentist. Coming up are first crushes, first heartbreaks, and first times behind the wheel of a car. I hope to someday see them each happily married with children of their own. Then I will gain entry into that even more exclusive sorority of "grandmotherhood."

For now, the password to my heart is "Mom," and I thank my sons for this. Especially on the days of their birth, happily on a special Sunday in May. My young sons do not yet realize how much I value this remarkable membership and won't note it with flowers unless prompted. Yet every time we take a walk, they pluck me a short-stemmed blossom, "just because."

This year I look forward to celebrating Mother's Day — the divine achievement of the physical, the grand acceptance of the commonplace, the exquisite gratitude of watching my sons become uniquely themselves. Because of Gabriel and Jordan, I am a dues-paying, card-carrying member of The Club. Happy Mother's Day to me!

Mimi's Kitchen

By Diana von Welanetz Wentworth

My mother loved being in the kitchen — it was her sanctuary. Like most families of the time, we ate the same foods over and over on a semi-regular rotation: spaghetti with tomato sauce, pot roast with mashed potatoes and gravy, tamale pie, fried chicken with mashed potatoes and gravy, roast leg of lamb with mint sauce and pan-roasted potatoes, and Polynesian spare ribs with pineapple, garlic and soy sauce. But we didn't mind the repetition, for along with the spices and seasoning, Mimi added that one special ingredient that only a mother could add — love.

Our shared moments in Mimi's kitchen and

the flavors and aromas of her repertoire of menus stay with me to this day. Mimi would tie an apron around me and ask me to shell and chop the walnuts for her fudge (still the best), which we packed in tins and kept in the antique French bombé chest in the dining room. My brother and I had permission to help ourselves.

But I was happiest when my mother made her spaghetti sauce for dinner. While the tangy tomato sauce simmered and splattered all over the white enamel stove-top, I would spoon a little into a saucer, open the freezer right next to the stove and place it on top of the frozen vegetables (lima beans — yuck!), close the door and wait restlessly until it was cool enough to taste. We still smile about the time I ate so much sauce there wasn't enough left for dinner! I was surprised I didn't get in trouble for it.

It was my job to hold the bundle of dried spaghetti and insert it into the huge kettle of boiling water (with a thin film of butter on top to prevent boiling over); I liked to watch the thin strands fall against the sides of the pot like a burst of the sun's rays.

A few years ago, Mimi gave me the greatest gift I can imagine. The family was gathered in the living room, but she and I were alone in the kitchen. She took my arm and said,

"Come with me, I need to tell you something." She led me to her pantry where we could speak privately. Mimi took both my hands and looked into my eyes. "Listen to me carefully, darling girl. You have been the most wonderful daughter any mother could ask for. I am more proud of you than I can ever say. When I'm gone, I want you to promise me you won't spend one moment feeling guilty about me! I've spent years feeling guilty about my mother — about things I didn't think to do for her…words I didn't say. I always wished I had done more for her — I just didn't know how.

"I've decided I don't want you to ever feel guilty about me for even one moment. You have been perfect and you have nothing to feel guilty for. Promise me!"

I promised. That moment became one of the great treasures of my life — absolved by my mother of all my failings!

Mimi, my dear mother — her presence has permeated every moment of my life. She is 89 now. I dread losing her, not having her nearby or physically available. But her spirit will live on in all I do. And so will her spaghetti sauce and the best fudge in the world.

Children
on
Loan

By Norma R. Larson

I am not good at returning things. Take library books. I have no intention of keeping them, but it takes a jolt to separate us — like a call from the librarian. Today, they sit awaiting return three days early. Because today, I'm painfully aware of the passage of time. In thirty minutes, assuming my son is packed — and he will be — Christopher Paul ("the best boy of all," he'd tease his sisters) leaves for his last year of college. He's our youngest, the last to leave home. By now, I tell myself, I am used to these departures. I am used to these departures. I am used to these departures…

Only this one is for keeps. Next May, there will be no bags of soiled laundry coming home. Chris won't be coming home at all. After graduation, it's marriage to Pam — the sunny Californian, adorable and already beloved by us all — and on to start their life together a thousand miles away. Every tick of our copper kitchen clock says, *This — is — it. Emp — ty — nest.*

My sister, the research chemist, calls. "For Pete's sake, you knew it was coming."

"So is the end of the world, but who's ready for it?"

"You really are in a mood."

My silence speaks for itself. Who knows us

as well as our sisters?

"After all," she adds, "he'll be home for the holidays. Anyway, you wouldn't want to keep him forever."

My sister does not read me well at all. I find myself caressing my chunky Timex as tenderly as I would a newborn's head. We've ticked away a lot of time together — waiting outside schools, athletic fields, piano lessons, rehearsals, practices. Later, awake in bed, listening for his first car to pull into the drive. Waiting as time dragged by. Now, in take-off time, seconds spring ahead.

The doorbell summons me to a girl selling candy for her school band. The six chocolate

bars are my excuse to visit Chris's room with
him still in it. Boxes block the doorway. A bar-
ricade? Walls easily erect themselves at times
like these. At his "Hi, Mom," I try to read his
voice. Glad I'm here? Resentful of intrusion?

He's tossing items into a carton labeled
MED.CAB.SUPPLIES. Glancing down on
stomach soothers, skin scrubbers, lens solu-
tion, musky colognes, I'm reminded of the
bottle of cheap aftershave he was so thrilled to
find in his stocking one long-ago Christmas.
He used it up in a week, but his room reeked
all winter. "Ever try this?" he asks now,
holding up a new brand of tooth gel. I smile
brightly as I shake my head, but I have the

ugly urge to snatch his alien brand and write
TRAITOR on his suitcase. We all use Crest.
We've always used Crest!

I realize my hand still clutches a damp
tissue when I find myself using it to wipe
his battered alarm clock. A wasted effort.
Not only is it no longer smeared with peanut
butter or sticky with Coke, I notice it is
among the abandoned.

"This still dependable?"

"Never failed me yet."

Which means just fifteen minutes to go.
"Time for a quick cup of coffee?" I would
climb a Brazilian mountain and hand-pick
beans to buy more time.

"Sure." He smiles in the lopsided way I love. He'll make a handsome bridegroom, but I really didn't have that in mind when I nagged him into slimming down in eighth grade.

It's been a long time since I stood watching coffee perk. I remember putting his early bottle on to warm, then starting the coffee. We snuggled cheek to cheek, waiting for our morning brews. He was warm with baby-sleep, I with mother-love. Neither of us minded the wait.

Now, sitting across from Chris as I gulp from my hot mug, I have to content myself with coffee and conversation. As appreciative as I am for our small talk, I'm aware of resenting it. More meaningful words could be said. I see by his watch that it's time for him to go. His hands are exactly like my father's. Odd I never noticed before. What else have I missed?

His eyes grow sober as he begins to speak of yesterday and seeing Pam off to her college, how they worked at keeping it light. I detect a message here for me, too. God knows I'm trying. And I wouldn't mind a little help from the Man Upstairs right now. You got me into this, I tell him. You let me share in your birthing business, but you messed up on the motherhood bit — or else I didn't read the fine print at the end.

"Well…" Chris stands and shoves in his chair. Never once has he shoved in his chair. "Now it's This is it, old chair. So long, old kitchen, old mother…"

I stand, too, but let my chair be. He bends over and gives me a kiss. It's always a sweet surprise, the firm kiss that shows he's not afraid of affection between us. Does he know how much it means?

"Hey… I'll call once I'm settled," he says, and his sensitivity triggers my tears.

"I really am trying to keep it light," I choke out with a tight laugh.

"Mom, it isn't as though…"

"I know. I know."

Three minutes A.D.— After Departure — I've blown my nose, repaired my make-up and am armed with my books. As I head for the door, my eyes happen to light on the plaque above it. It's hung there for years, overlooked as we hastily, purposefully, moved through our lives as a family. The line from Tennyson must have been waiting for just this moment.

God gives us love. Something to love, he lends us.

Children on loan. And I've never been good at returning things.

In a

Hurry

By Gina Barrett Schlesinger

I was in a hurry.

I came rushing through our dining room in my best suit, focused on getting ready for an evening meeting. Gillian, my four-year-old, was dancing about to one of her favorite oldies, "Cool," from *West Side Story*.

I was in a hurry, on the verge of being late. Yet a small voice inside of me said, *Stop*.

So I stopped. I looked at her. I reached out, grabbed her hand and spun her around. My seven-year-old, Caitlin, came into our orbit, and I grabbed her, too. The three of us did a wild jitterbug around the dining room and into the living room. We were laughing. We were spinning. Could the neighbors see the lunacy through the windows? It didn't matter. The song ended with a dramatic flourish and our dance finished with it. I patted them on their bottoms and sent them to take their baths.

They went up the stairs, gasping for breath, their giggles bouncing off the walls. I went back to business. I was bent over, shoving papers into my briefcase, when I overheard my youngest say to her sister, "Caitlin, isn't Mommy the bestest one?"

I froze. How close I had come to hurrying through life, missing that moment. My mind went to the awards and diplomas that covered the walls of my office. No award, no achievement I have ever earned can match this: *Isn't Mommy the bestest one?*

My child said that at age four. I don't expect her to say it at age 14. But at age 40, if she bends down over that pine box to say good-bye to the cast-off container of my soul, I want her to say it then.

Isn't Mommy the bestest one?

It doesn't fit on my résumé. But I want it on my tombstone.